# Mo(u)rning Rituals

# Mo(u)rning Rituals

Poems by

Heidi Slettedahl

Cover image by Heidi Slettedahl
Author photo by Zach Lyman

ISBN: 978-1-63980-599-0
Library of Congress Control Number: 2024940455

Kelsay Books
502 South 1040 East, A-119
American Fork, Utah 84003
Kelsaybooks.com

For Allan, always

# Acknowledgments

Grateful acknowledgement is made to the editors of the following publications in which these pieces first appeared (some in earlier versions):

*Autumn Sky Daily:* "Mo(u)rning Rituals"
*Before I Leave:* "When I Weep"
*Black Coffee Review:* "The Words Unspoken"
*Black Poppy Review:* "Follow Me"
*Crosscurrents:* "Destinations," "The Seduction"
*Discretionary Love:* "Beloved," "Love Doesn't Live in a Hotel Room"
*Dream Noir:* "Loneliness," "The River's Edge"
*Ink, Sweat and Tears:* "Flowers and Baguettes"
*Literary Mama:* "Rummage Sale"
*Lothlorien Poetry Journal:* "Final Clearance," "Paper Calendars," "The Cycle," "Untitled"
*Not Very Quiet:* "The Bus"
*Panoplyzine:* "A Gratitude Stone"
*Picaroon Poetry:* "My Children"
*Rag Mag:* "Absence," "Housebound"
*The Red Eft Review:* "ICU," "Rear View Mirror," "The Alphabet Game," "A Day That Lost Its Meaning," "Venice"
*right hand pointing Moral Injury Project:* "Lavender Burned Black"
*Synaeresis:* "My Phantom Child"
*Taste:* "For M."
*Tipton Poetry Journal:* "The Lake"
*Visual Verse:* "Catching the Moment," "Of All the Ways," "The Menu," "A Place of Death"
*Vita Brevis Literature:* "Pots"

# Contents

Part III

# Part I

# My Children

I never got to teach my children anything.
A mass of cells that multiplied
And then did not
No long division
No make believe

Except those two weeks, waiting.

Each time was harder
And every time I knew.

# Mo(u)rning Rituals

In my arms she is an accustomed weight and almost
carelessly transferred,
my right hip jutting out, my white blouse creased
in patterns her kicking heel repeats.

It is the carelessness that gives away the dream.

She is hot against me, leaning too close, reaching.
I shake away her grasping fingers, her urge to crook a pinkie
in the perfect gold hoop in my ear,
                                    tug
                                        down.

Looking at someone else, I talk above her,
sensing only gradually my arm asleep beneath me,
her sticky heat a damp mattress in a hot and sunny room.

Her weight disperses as she fades.

I grope for a thin glass cylinder, shaken down, muting me.

He stirs beside me, sees the spear in my mouth,
and shuts his eyes again.

I hate this ritual.
*Not yet, not yet.*
Not ever.

I cannot think that and I do, my thoughts helpless partners tied
by the wrists, facing outwards,
facing away.
To pull against is to tighten the knots.

His hands reach for me          I shake my head.
*No,* I say, *it's not time,* I say.

I think he is relieved.

Today, I think, I will not conjure her; she will not fill the spaces
in my day.
Today, I promise,
I will not recall that careless weight, a conversation that goes on
above her head.

It is the carelessness I crave,
the fact she is not central to my dream.

# Housebound

Tie me to my home with a dog or a child
Bind me with promises of leisure
I can help you tie the knots
I can't refuse
You are doing this for
me only me
I learn to cook meals of sumptuous delight for
you only you

I arrange the flowers just so
The windows sparkle every day   The glare keeps me
From looking out
Finally I'm the shape a mother should be
who tucks you in at night
afraid to ask you where you've been

# My Phantom Child

Failure is signified by blood
my blood

The phantom kickings that never were
slide out with blood and cramps and tears

such a damn familiar sight, this puffy face, the one I want to see
transformed,
my phantom child, with eyes like mine and hair that curls
just like your father's does, when it is damp. He
pushes at it fiercely, keeps it short to straighten it

Your pudgy fingers, ten in all, and perfect crescent fingernails
They're real, so real to me I've felt contractions in my sleep,
the urge to push, to grunt and to expel
to *want* the pain your birth produces
to welcome it, a pain
        that ends (not like this one) miraculously.

# Expulsion

Three times she felt expulsion
and the years, confined to talk not conversation
made trying first impossible to bear, then hard to stop.
Meant that the fleshy space inside she's never seen
remained unoccupied, and shed each month as so much waste.

# Rummage Sale

Baby clothes. Get there early or they go.

The woman in charge has her back to the table,
the reason everyone has come.
Jumpsuits, onesies, bibs and bonnets
Mostly yellow as if she didn't really want to know.

Unusual, this restraint, a throwback even.
No gender reveal, no party thrown, no extra gifts.

Baby Clothes (Unworn).

The sign itself
(And the parenthesis of course)
Stop me briefly

Long enough to lose out to another mother,
quicksilver thief,

owner now of something perfect,
something imagined

Something lost.

# Venice

I rarely talk about my babies
Eight in all,
The loss too large for casual conversation.

Eight that I am sure of.
Who wants to know of clinics and injections, and odds
you'd never bet on
Until you do.

The number might be nine, if I include
The one who left me in Venice
With blood and chills.

At least I think he did, if he was there at all.
So hard to know for sure.

My friends love Venice,
Return to it year on year.

I prefer Verona.
A smaller city, prettier, less crowded.

Fewer memories of loss.

# Beloved

With someone else I might have had a child.

He might have had one, too.
(I tuck the thought away.)

My beloved child, imagined so repeatedly I can see
curls in her hair, a defiant stance.
She is small and mighty,
thus literary and not mine.

With each other we wrestle with love and regrets

The tiny aches that bloom and die and bloom again.

Will always bloom again.

# The Words Unspoken

The words unspoken
Are too precious to say out loud.

We held him briefly.
Took no photos home.

My memories of him are all
I need to hold.

# Choosing

They chose haphazardly that first time,
Who should sit where.
She chose the opposite side she had for the bed,
Not out of conscious choice,
but rather, the position of the sun.

Now, thirty years later, houses later, here they still sit,
No children
No musical chairs
Just this: a station determined, a seat claimed.

Drinking coffee, the sun shining over his left eye
so that he has to squint
He only sees the outlines of her.
She looks back at the man she thinks he is.
And neither quite remembers the gloriousness of first love
New love
Or even the reason for choosing.

# Love Doesn't Live in a Hotel Room

It lives in the kitchen
In the cracks in the floor
In the time it takes a dishwasher to be emptied
In a gas tank filled
In a bed made
In a garden tended by one who hates the weeds.

# Part II

# Flowers and Baguettes

Her shopping trolley thought she had the kind of life
where flowers and baguettes would feature regularly.

She was just shopping for detergent and descaler.

She wanted to live up to this imagined life,
even sometimes bought such flowers, such baguettes,
They wilted early
or went stale
Such things were meant to be shared.

To fool her loyalty card she also bought
wildly inappropriate things:
baby wipes, dog biscuits, meals for two.

She wanted a more complex and chaotic life.

Flowers and baguettes didn't work with this life either.
But after all, this was on different days
For different audiences.

# The Menu

The menu offered hope, before he arrived
the man she couldn't imagine fully
a man her brother's best friend's cousin knew, once.

He was running late.

She'd never had ostrich, but knew it was like a very tender beef
her brother's best friend's cousin told her, once.
She thought she'd try it someday. Maybe now.

If he was a vegetarian, she'd lose points she couldn't afford to lose.

She could try a salad, beets and goat's cheese, caramelized pecans
Dressed lightly, perhaps with dressing on the side
and a granary roll with salted butter.

Unless he was a vegan.

She's not sure why she cares.
She didn't dress up.
She didn't dress down.

She sits, with the menu, pondering her choice.

# Catching the Moment

You'll get your hair wet, she said,
Though it was her fault I was leaning over
Her voice so soft I had to use my eyes to hear.
I had to try to read her lips to understand.

She told me things I already knew:
I didn't match.
I was too much
I'd never find her
I wasn't loved

They only caught the moment of my stooping.
They never caught the moment of my rise.

# Of All the Ways

Of all the ways to weigh herself
This was the least convenient.
First the long walk through the field,
The gate to move
The skirt to hitch up just so,
The leap to land legs first.

It almost never worked.

And when it did, there was never anyone there to see or to applaud.

She tried it anyway, but only in the summer.

It passed the time.
It reminded her of the times she flew with grace and light,
Trapeze after trapeze and arms outstretched and hardly ever
dropped.

# In Flight

She didn't lose her tongue
She let it loose
A cacophony of words flying out of her
Some of which she regretted
The rest of which came back to perch on her lips
Or flew away into the clouds
And made it rain.

# This Is How Your Friendship Ends

You move away.
You get married.
She has kids. You don't.

You get busy.
She gets busy.
You don't call.

You make a choice,
A hurtful choice.
You turn away.

You don't turn back.

# Loneliness

Loneliness
a white sheet
drawn over me at night,
my naked body
unaccustomed to the weight

# When I Weep

I find I skip to years
and forget the days, the one by one
the alcoholic pledge.
All colors swirl to one,
a mucky brown on paper.
All colors swirl from white
and back again, if we but see it.
I only see the brown.
I argue with the future and forget
that days have red and streaks of blue
and gentle curving arms that hold me
when I weep.

# My Sister Told Me

My sister told me
The vampires come at night
You have to cover your neck to keep safe

I wore a scarf to bed for years
Still do except on nights I'm brave

I'm not often very brave

But now I know she's wrong.
The vampires come in the light.

You just don't see them
For what they are
Until it is too late.

# For M.

I have known nights of your strangled, sleepy voice.

> *I almost died tonight.*
> *I couldn't breathe. My heart—*

You are twenty-two, I say, bewildered,
wondering what to make of your body grown old,
forced into wrinkles and heart palpitations.

> *Granola works the best.*
> *But sometimes, the smell of urine is enough.*
> *I put my nose right down into the bowl.*
> *Afterwards, I rest my forehead on the lid*
> *and I am proud.*

You were happy I finally knew,
delirious with details of how and when.

You clung to me like Saran Wrap.
You sucked into me like I was your food.

# Eve

It isn't men who cry
who so offend the sensibilities,
it's men who learn it, calculating a soft
exterior and harbouring anger against Eve
who after all is allowed her tears
(but don't forget her pain)
and who created pain initially, eating
that apple, planting that seed and forcing
Adam, a man who didn't cry, to go along with her.

It's men like these who forget
the anger of being tricked belongs to Eve
not Adam, belongs to a woman who hears a seductive
voice, a sensual one which promises oh so much.
Can she be blamed for watching tears indifferently
when she remembers Adam and his rage?

# A Place of Death

Let's make this harder, he said,
taking the Rubik's Cube from me, a puzzle I had almost solved.
It was his mantra, always, *harder.*
I let him place the triangle in my hand,
the triangle that was not a triangle, a name I couldn't grasp.
Prism? Pyramid? A place of death?
The shape felt so good in my hand, as I turned it,
the colors reminding me of *Promising Young Woman.*
A film I didn't like,
a film soaked in pastels, making the images feminine and soft.
And deadly.
*Let's make this harder,* he said.
It was hard enough already.
It was time to put the object down.

# Follow Me

Follow me, will you?
Watch my movement and my ways with averted eyes
pretending.

You are a child,
my size.

You frighten me.

*I've been waiting for you.*

The words, so sinister,
drop from enchanting lips
another has kissed and set aside.

Am I to be punished for her cruelty?
She laughed at you *oh god how could she*
She mimicked you, she taunted you, *the bitch!*

She deserves to be punished, yes to die
She will.
Today.
Tomorrow, too.

She dies daily.
Her corpse has a hundred different faces,
Faces shocked and still.
No longer laughing.
No longer crying.
Not at you.

# The Seduction

We dove
hand and hand
into the swimming pool.
We broke the surface
with laughing approval.
Will you be my lover?
He asks, gripping tighter to
my hand,
anticipating my response.
Oh yes,
I whisper, as we tread
water.
Will you be my lover?
He asks, clasping me
in his arms.
Oh yes,
I whisper, as we begin
to sink.
Will you be my lover?
He asks, as our lips
sink beneath the surface.
Oh yes,
I whisper as I gasp
for breath.
Will you be my lover?
He asks, as he envelopes
me in his arms,
as he forces my lips apart.
Oh yes, I struggle as
our toes touch the bottom.

Will you be my lover?
He asks, as he brings me
further down.
Will you be my lover?
NO! I explode, as I
try to spring from the bottom of the pool.
No! I counter, as he holds
more tightly to me.
You're drowning me! I shudder
as I gasp for breath.
I struggle to the surface,
my lover close to my side.
I'm leaving you! I gasp
as we break the surface.
I see the panic in his eyes
as he says
Let go! You're drowning
me! My lover's eyelids
close as he sinks to
the bottom of
the pool.

# Pots

One by one the pots get broken,
hurled off the ledge

by wind, not violence
and the helpful hand of a garden chair upturned.

Earth finds its way to earth,
slabs of concrete breaking the journey.
Old roots lie exposed.

The rain comes at the wrong time
Too soon to shift the dirt
Too muddy now to rescue flowers turned upside down

Instant gratification gardener
Instantly unearthed

# I See My Hands

Each time I see a new spot marking territory
The Ivory Liquid challenge comes to mind:
When youth was prized and women shamed for hands
that aged them.
Commercial of my youth, identify the mother and the daughter
Just by looking at their hands.
A false comparison
I see that now
But still it stuck.
I wore rubber gloves to do the dishes
Lotioned them daily
And still the age spots betrayed me.
I see my hands
No daughter's to compare them to
I see my hands.

# The Breadmaker

Is it her or the machine?
She'll take the credit, the loaf so beautiful and light.
Only the hole torn in the bottom to confirm
A less than truthful claim.

# The Visitor

The visitor surprised me,
barring entrance to my home.
I paused before deciding to swing
the door inside.
He watched, unperturbed.

Escaped or released I couldn't tell.
Knowing he wouldn't survive the frost
Knowing he'd travelled too far to return
I shut him out.

# The Ankle

It is scarred where a bicycle's spokes
grabbed and caught the wrinkled flesh.
Now, years later, it has forgotten the trip.
It moves as if to tap
a piano's pedal
and then retreats.

# The Basement

The piano's in the basement
Next to the brown shower curtain
That blocks the view of Dad's old workshop.
The water heater harmonizes
Thumps of footsteps getting closer.
My grandmother taught me to sing to mask
The noise
Loudly and off key
But my eyes still stray to the curtain that sways
From an invisible breeze.

# Christmas Angel

I start with the head
The wings are next
The body I save for last, the amorphous part, clothed in robes
and sugar sprinkles,
Fat with deliciousness
Satisfying and obscene.

# The Game

She weaned herself off games slowly,
As she had with caffeine.
Still, temptation struck each day
Taunting her with memories of the rush
Of success
Of prizes won.
It never disappeared,
Always lingered on the edge of consciousness
Calling her seductively
Seeking her company again.

# Promises I will never keep

Stop playing Candy Crush
Work out more
Use my time wisely
Write
Call my mother
Be nicer to my dog

# Be Careful

Be careful!
The words are always spoken too late,
After the awkward step
Just before the fall

Be careful!
We say it like a mantra
to ward the blame off us
And onto those who didn't listen

# Travel with Me

Looking out the window of the plane
all I can think is how vast
America is

How easy
to hide a body.

The thrillers I read while traveling travel with me.

# Destinations

She bought maps of places
she would never go,
huge multicolored maps,
taped unevenly on the walls, filled
with red lines of travel
and destinations marked with X's.

# America

We decided to fly the flags permanently at half mast.
It was easier than taking away the guns.

# A Gratitude Stone

*South Africa, February 2010*

Simple words like legacy,
passion, commitment, love.
Things we say about ourselves
but might not always mean
writ large against a wall
in sparse cool language
embossed or etched in stone
          or blood.

I've told you things I haven't said to family,
my legacy so much in doubt and fear.

How do we move from prisons
to talking about ourselves
and make it meaningful?

I offer you a prayer
or carry your camera
or ask for pictures of your son.

My only gift is reaching out.
The wisdom of the prison—
A gratitude stone.

# No Photos Required

No photos required for happy memories.
Yet I regret the failure to pause
To capture
To arrange just so
Missing out on permanence that way

In my memory she laughs with purple hair,
Or practices a stern face as her husband lets slip a past indiscretion
A small one
A party jape
I see her perfecting the look
He perfects mock shame

It's years since she wore purple in her hair
My memories overlay each other
Blurring the lines
But not the moment
No photos required for happy memories.
They stick like jelly on the floor.

# Absence

I touch you with words
because my hands cannot reach you
over there      across miles of water
land
I reach back for you
through dreams and memories
and tv shows that recall our shared
and unshared past.

My life      bound up with another's now
and bountiful
happy often    painful too
holds your absence closely    makes of it
a presence      and a voice

# Sister

In my letters I tell you
      privately
in conversations over
      thin black wires
      over watery waves I cannot count
You are my friend,
my best friend.

      You share my soul
like no one can
not even him I live with

I think of miles and miles and miles
      and my choice to leave you
choosing between my life
      and my life
choosing him because I knew
      that you would wait for me

# Haunting

You became a ghost too soon
and how you haunt me     you
lightly touch my arm
make an indentation on my bed
slip past my vision     hover at the corners
like a mother who doesn't want to hover
like a lover whose presence demands attention
silently.
No footsteps     no slamming doors     no crying softly
these are human things
that need no ghostly presence.

# Paper Calendars

I cling to paper calendars
Note the birthdays of those I love

Forget to send them cards.

I trace the oddity of this year
For one year only
there is a week for every year of my life.

I've never used them up before.

And next year I'll double back
Count one week twice

Each year adds more duplicity.

The way the calendar forces 1 and 31 to share a line
To keep the rows an even four,
Form more essential than clarity,

Contained duplicity the goal.

# Reading for Pleasure

I say I don't read anymore
But I read the posts
The nasty things that people say
About me
About others
I inhale it
I wheeze and inhale again.

What I wouldn't give for a sentence that shines
Not someone who sentences me

# You Can Look Me Up

And isn't that a thing to say
You can find the people who like to proclaim their public hate
One click and you're there
A digital version of me who isn't me
But who is replicated to infinity

Did I sign up for this?
If so I can't recall

# Part III

# I Prefer White Wine

I'll drink red with my sister
Sitting out on the porch
Talking about old memories
Good times
The things we never tell to others.

# The Cycle

Trapped in a cycle of regret
my mother clings to slights
imagined or real,
decisions made she wants to reverse,
anxious over judgments offered
when her children were young and burdensome.

# Lavender Burned Black

We burned it, my sister and I
that note you wrote on lavender paper.
The lavender burned black and fell apart.

You slapped me when you saw
the purple black ashes
but I was numb to the tingle and neither of us cried.

Oh mother, mother, I don't want to know
of wrinkled sheets and whispered conversations
and feel the pain of trying not to love you.

But I will not forgive the evenings
you were gone, the days
my father spent in anger, mending the cracks

in the house's foundation
pounding the nails into soft, pliant wood
drinking warm beer

while you cooked dinner in tense, frustrated silence
we all ignored
until your anger flashed and caught me with your tongue.

You taught me lessons even in your silence,
the dance of avoidance, the masquerade.
The anger

lingers in that house you left.
It sits in the corners with the heavy dust,
A guest we don't dare disturb.

The anger follows you,
reminds you of the ashes of your love letter
and the daughters who burned the words you wrote.

Its tendrils grasp for me
as I realize my handwriting mirrors yours.
Oh how the anger flashes when I see I write those letters too.

# M.F.E.O.

*He was the love of my life.*
She says this after her third glass of wine.
She pours them big these days. In truth she always has.

*What will I do? What will I do?*
Her voice is familiar, intoxicated.
Performed?
It would be wrong of me to say.

I have no comfort.
I have impatience.
I push it back to no effect, my memories too vivid
to dull with wine.

It's not like this is the first time I've heard this speech,
though the other two were ugly splits, with living men.
My father.
Number two, whose name we do not say.
And now.

M.F.E.O.
They signed their cards that way, channeling *Sleepless in Seattle,*
a film I never liked.
Made For Each Other.
Even when we saw forced smiles and bright eyes,
Even after accidental butt dials, indistinguishable words and tears,
tears, tears,
Words that blurred and slurred and could not be made out.
Words that daughters shouldn't be made to listen to.

M.F.E.O
My fucking egotistical other.

# You Are Beautiful

My mother's book awaits me
calling forth for praise and understanding

I have little of both having lived through life with her.

She shows me her new dentures,
wants praise for how they change her.
I think of my father and his early joke,
the note that they were not meant to be:

I look like a rabbit, she said

No, no, he replied. Your ears are too short.

She preens to me and I say
You are beautiful
What else can I say
What else does she want to hear
Her ears are too small to hear anything else

# A Day That Lost Its Meaning

How do you celebrate a day that lost its meaning?
My parents' wedding anniversary, unmarked,

no calendar line reminding me.
And yet, it nudges a fleeting thought,
a memory of cards once made or bought

The end date unremarked and unrecalled in specificity:
a date in May not emblazoned in my heart.

# Scavenger

My father is a scavenger
who stops the car for every roadside flash of metal.
He returns from walks with scarves
and aluminium cans.
Once, he found fifty cents
inside a soft-sided cigarette carton.
He bought me popcorn with it,
to feed the ducks.

His workshop struggles under mismatched plywood
tins of nails,
sandpaper,                table saws.
At the mall, he takes me to Sears
and shows me the tools he wants to buy.

He goes to coffee every afternoon at three
to roll the dice,
telling jokes he heard in 1945.
He knows one line of every song.

He is a mailman whose bifocaled eyes spot
every eagle and hawk on his rural route.

On Sundays when I'm home he takes me out to breakfast,
to drink his coffee slowly,
to show me his newest treasure,
to tell me news that can't wait for a letter.

# The Lottery

My dad tells me every time he wins the lottery,
The hundred dollar gain,
The smaller wins.
He thrills at the money, he makes sure I know
It was worth it, the effort, the ticket, the waiting in line.

Days go by without us speaking.

# My Father's Words

Don't use your car as an overcoat
I see my boss's startled face
And laugh
A little
Put on a self-deprecating smile

My father said that to me often
The voice comes out of me unbidden

He shrugs and ignores my advice

My father's voice
Which speaks to me alone.

# ICU

The first trip was after midnight.
Woken from a sort of sleep, I hesitated.
Couldn't figure out what to wear.
What do you wear?

The second time I didn't delay.
Got into the car almost as I was.
Hungry, I seem to recall.

The vending machine didn't work.
I stayed without a fix of sugar, fat, salt.
Hunger in a waiting room, then next to him,
who also wasn't eating.

Each time I enter more disheveled.
Each time his breath is less secure.

Did I do this the wrong way around?
Shouldn't it become easier and clearer?
Shouldn't I offer a more presentable face?
Be more ready?

You would have thought
I've had enough practice by now.

# The Alphabet Game

In the absence of billboards I always find the same J.
A sullen part of the journey, the Adopt-a-Highway sign
my only savior.
I don't remember the name, just that it's there,

In memory of someone.

Enough to push me past the tricky letter, on.
Road construction and closed lanes,
a truck always in front, always slow, impossible to pass.

Kay Ell Emm Enn Oh Pee

I listen to the radio, as it secures its sound and then retreats,
impossible to hold
until the exit to Rochester,
where the Qs and Xs and Zs are easy to find

I always get to the end before I stop,
liquor stores and plazas helping out.
A left at Mayo, a right to parking.
They trust the families to pay the fees, at night.

Sometimes I pretend I've been there less time than I have,
Shave a half an hour off the fee,
The envelope still heavy with quarters and fat with dollar bills.

Sometimes I don't pay at all.
Leave the honor system behind.
Become the bad girl I never was.

If you knew you'd be there daily, you'd buy the weekly pass.
I should have bought the weekly pass.
I wish there were a monthly one.

I wish that I would need it.

# History Lesson

My father teaches me that time is not linear
It loops

It's not the lesson he means to teach.

He wants to teach me history
His history

The things no one else writes down.

# Untitled

Right back here again
In the icky in between

Booking flights to see the sights
We do not want to see:
Tubes, monitors, hospital beds

Diminished body
Diminished mind

My dad.

# In Pieces

Swung high above his head I heard my father say
*I love you to pieces.*
Oh Dad, I said, I love you together.

A three year old's response, repeated often in my house,
to laughter.
I remember the moment.

I remember being told about the moment.
It's the same result: a memory.

I love you to pieces
I love you together

Each month the pieces come apart.
Each week a little weaker
No more swinging arms above his head

No more walking.
no more.

Daddy, daddy, I love you together.

And I am in pieces now.

# The River's Edge

I've never swum in a river
for fear of tides
and my dead uncle.

My father made us learn to swim in pools
even as he stood on the edge, himself unable.

Vacations, my mother left with her sister, shopping, while
my father stood guard at the pool.
I think of it now.
He was helpless, should anything have gone wrong.
But still he stayed.
He watched.
He toweled us off when we were done.

But rivers were forbidden.
I think of that now, on the river's edge
as I pour his ashes slowly in.

# The Lake

You don't see the colors of the lake
Until you take the photograph
Subtle shades of pink and gray
And underneath it all the swimming fish
The seaweed that tangles your ankles
The last breath of someone that you love.

# Final Clearance

Eventually someone will go through this place too
Deciding what to throw and what to keep
What deserves a second life
What does not

I won't be there to direct the future
Explain the past
The gap will have to be just that
A gap

We think we'll know and can prepare
We never can

A house is just a house
And stuff is stuff

And books (oh books!)
Remain unread

# The Bus

Outside it is snowing, and not a little bit,
The kind that makes you want to stay indoors,
The kind that gets down the neck of your coat if you are not,
that clings and melts against your skin.
The kind that is lovely in December and truly awful in March,
The kind that makes the car slide out from under you, towards
that tree,
or that ditch or worse yet
that person, just standing there, waiting for the bus.

# Rear View Mirror

The soft edges of a dream tease
at me while I awaken.
A child in a short cotton dress,
rosy pink with grass stains on the hem,
clasps her hand in another's
as they cross the street,
a line of children daring traffic.

Her partner lets go.

Her hand slips to the pavement,
dusty sand burrows in her knees.
Sprouts of blood dampen the gravely ground
and the car that's approaching doesn't stop

doesn't stop

The edges of the dream are fading.
The shadow of the car
that brushed my consciousness
has driven away.
The driver permitted one slow last gaze,

My eyes are blurry from slumber
and I cannot recognize the face.

# The Horizon

He tells me he only has to live a few more years.
Get me to retirement.
Then I can live where I want.

The words are matter of fact and his eyes are at the horizon
As if he is already tracking his death.
As if he can actually see it coming.

We re-upped, I say.
You remember. At 25 years I said I'd sign on for 25 more
But after that you're on your own.

He squeezes my hand.
The dog jerks the leash and he moves towards the pull
Correcting her path,

Keeping her from doing her business on the neighbor's lawn.
We don't know them.
We can't allow our mess to show up there.

The moment's passed and now a row of houses blocks our vision
The horizon no longer visible
The topic closed, for now.

# Being Burned

I want to be burned.
Though unlike paper, bodies are not easily destroyed.
(Oh how the image pleases me.)

The benefit of childlessness:
I don't have to think about your feelings.
There's no one to remember me.

How comforting to know
I am not bigger than I am.
I don't have to outlast this life.

# About the Author

Heidi Slettedahl is an academic and a US-UK dual national who goes by a slightly different name professionally. In her other life, she is President of SUNY Brockport. Her love of creative writing was nurtured early by her English teachers (Mr. Nelson, Mr. Zumhofe, thank you) and by a chance encounter with the poet Nancy Paddock. It was at St. Cloud State University that she really embraced her craft, and she credits Dr. Steve Klepetar with opening her eyes and her mind to writing more fully. (She is also forever grateful that he wrote a poem for her presidential inauguration.) She lives in western New York with her husband Allan Macpherson and their two unruly Springer Spaniels, Tilly and Rosie. Her most unusual talent is her ability to ride a unicycle. She does less of that now that she is over 50.

Printed in the USA
CPSIA information can be obtained
at www.ICGtesting.com
CBHW030741080924
14152CB00011B/325